BAMBOO FLY ROD SUITE

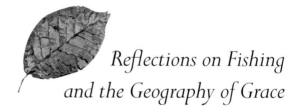

*Reflections on Fishing
and the Geography of Grace*

BAMBOO FLY ■ ROD ■ SUITE

Frank Soos

■ ■ ■

Illustrations by
Kesler Woodward

The University of Georgia Press
Athens and London

Published by the University of Georgia Press
Athens, Georgia 30602
© 1999 by Frank Soos
Illustrations © 1999 by Kesler Woodward
All rights reserved

Designed by Wanda W. Chin
Set in 13/16 Perpetua with Colonna display
Printed and bound by C & C Printing, Inc.
The paper in this book meets the guidelines for
permanence and durability of the Committee on
Production Guidelines for Book Longevity of the
Council on Library Resources.

Printed in Hong Kong

03 02 01 00 99   C   5 4 3 2 1

Library of Congress Cataloging in Publication Data

Soos, Frank.
Bamboo fly rod suite : reflections on fishing and the
geography of grace / Frank Soos ; illustrations by
Kesler Woodward.
p.   cm.
ISBN 0-8203-2064-1 (alk. paper)
1. Fishing rods. 2. Bamboo. 3. Consumer behavior—
Social aspects. 4. Consumption (Economics)—Social
aspects. 5. Imperfection. I. Title.
SH452.S66   1999
799.1—dc21   98-24841

British Library Cataloging in Publication Data available

For my mother, Genevieve N. Soos

CONTENTS

3 ■ ON WANTING EVERYTHING

23 ■ THE AGE OF IMPERFECTION

35 ■ USEFUL TOOLS

47 ■ ON HIS SLOWNESS

61 ■ OBITUARY WITH BAMBOO FLY ROD

BAMBOO FLY ROD SUITE

"You can only fish with one at a time," was what my mother said.

ON WANTING EVERYTHING

I thought I was as happy as I had any reason to expect to be. I was living in Alaska, teaching college English, making more money than I'd ever dreamed of making. I was just sitting in my office minding my own business. If anybody had asked me I might have said I was free of want, free of desire. One of the guys I work with, Eric Heyne, came by with a faded blue cardboard tube. I had a feeling—the kind of feeling you get when somebody you work with casually drops by in the middle of the day—that whatever he wanted was going to involve effort, a favor of some kind I was about to get roped into. I put on a dangerous face, dragged the corners of my mustache down. But Eric didn't seem to notice. He screwed the cap off the tube and pulled out a long brown sack, all the while talking about this bamboo fishing rod. I told him I didn't know anything about bamboo rods. Which was kind of true. I didn't know much except that with the possible exception of a BMW motorcycle there was no thing in the world I might have wanted more.

As a six-year-old in Virginia standing on the bank of the lake backed up behind Falls Mills Dam where my parents brought us to fish with our worms and bobbers, I saw a man—Dr. Ballard, our town's GP— as he stood in his flat-bottomed skiff casting a popping bug to the edge of a raft of lily pads. He had a sidearm delivery, and the long line whipped out toward me, snakily, enticingly, then pulled back, then came again. Then finally it settled itself on the flat water. Dr. Ballard flipped the tip of the rod, and from halfway across the lake I could hear the lure gurgle and pop. We had no boat, and I was too young to manage my casting reel, too inexperienced to ride my thumb on the arbor to prevent backlashes from building in my line. My dad cast for me, and I learned to watch my bobber and wait.

Eric had already taken the fly rod to a fishing tackle store where the guy had told him his pole was worthless. About all it was good for was a wall hanging, a conversation piece, something else to stick in the corner. Eric thought he had enough junk to stick in corners, and I said I did too. But he said I could have it if I wanted it, could take it in to another shop for a second opinion. I applied my mother's famous axiom: If somebody gives you something, take it; if they hit you, run.

Having this rod fall into my lap put me in the grasp of Reverend Ike, the Harlem preacher whose literature I'd seen left in my dad's store when I was a boy. He offered the Blessing Plan, or "Why wait for pie in the sky when you can have it now?" The way you got started in the Blessing Plan, something like a divinely ordained chain letter, was by mailing a faith offering to Reverend Ike. His brochure was filled with news of people who'd won cars in raffles, hit the jackpot at the bingo hall, received unexpected inheritances from relatives they didn't even know existed. There stood Reverend Ike in a full-color photograph, in his conked pompadour and brocade tuxedo jacket, proof incarnate of the good things waiting to come my way.

When I said I didn't know anything about bamboo rods, I was trying to slip out from under a responsibility I thought would come from telling the truth, that what I knew about bamboo rods was in the wanting. I had probably wanted one as long as I had been fly-fishing—since I was twelve years old. I'd never thought I'd own one because I had priced them in an Orvis catalogue. I can't remember how much they cost, only that the figure was beyond what I'd imagined ever paying for a fishing rod, or anything else my twelve-year-old self could conceive of wanting, for that matter.

Yet I did want such a rod. Laid out handsomely in the catalogue display, such rods invited me to take them up, to handle their cigar-shaped cork grips, their clean amber grain, and the lighter bursting nodes of the cane. I saw how in taking up such a rod I might be changed into the man in the boat. Hadn't that man himself been changed from the sometimes-sinister guy humming his little tune to cover the sounds of the sterilizer door clanking open and the hypodermic being prepared to some magical figure capable of standing up in a boat, of almost walking on water? Casting his fly rod, he had made himself beautiful. Beauty. It was a word you didn't hear much growing up in a coal camp.

Somewhere among the junk gathered in a catchall box on top of my dad's dresser there can still be found a key chain with a St. Christopher's medal and a key to the chained oars of a rowboat, a boat perpetually on loan to us during my high school years. Somewhere in a damp basement corner stands my dad's cheap fiberglass fly rod. I own a couple of cheap ones myself and one pretty good graphite rod. Now I even own a BMW bike, though it is covered by a plastic tarp and sitting on my aunt's porch back in Virginia. I have sought a narrow satisfaction of my wanting.

I took a closer look at the rod. The guides and tip-tops were rusting and some were missing from the fraying wraps. But it was all there, four pieces, two tips of the same length. *Shakespeare Au Sable* was printed on the tube and *Shakespeare* on the label on the butt section of the rod, and I knew Shakespeare. In the hillbilly fishing world of my boyhood, Shakespeare was top-of-the-line gear. Didn't Fuzzy Elmore himself use nothing but?

I took the rod home and put it in my basement. I left it there maybe four years without thinking about it too much. I think I left it alone for so long because I was a little afraid of it. What if Eric Heyne decided one day that he wanted this fishing rod back? What if in trying to make it fishable I only screwed it up? I thought of the rod in this way as something like an exhumed mammoth's tusk waiting to be carved. Once it was done, done well or done poorly, it was finished. There could only be so many out there, couldn't there? And finally, I wondered what if I did fix it all up and fished with it and liked it and *then* Eric came around and wanted it back? I thought I would be honor-bound to return it. Maybe it was better not to actually allow myself to own it at all but to just let it inhabit my house, a ghostly promise of all my fishing wishes.

Just recently, out fishing with my brother, I stepped into a river. Last time the water here had been knee-high. This time I found myself leaning against a swift current in water up to my chest. I felt myself losing touch with the bottom, becoming buoyant from the air trapped in my baggy waders. At such times, a feeling of panic comes over me; I feel it in the hair rising on my neck, in the blood rushing in my ears. I wonder if I just might become disconnected, float away.

I wondered if I wasn't being tugged toward the dark source of every ugly human impulse. This is what Reverend Ike tapped into without fully knowing what he'd discovered. Greed. Greed is what made this country great, of course. It's what built the railroads and the factories. But if that's the case, it was part of a two-stroke engine. On one hand, a robber baron went out and pillaged our resources and broke the backs of his workers. On the other, he got to feeling bad about it and built libraries and endowed symphony orchestras. Usually the guilt came after the getting, and usually the libraries and orchestra halls were named for the benefactor.

From its start, the history of our country has been peopled with plenty of oily, greedy preachers too. But what Reverend Ike did was advance this age-old type through a small adjustment with major consequences. Before, the preacher, pernicious or not, told the gullible flock to sit down and take it. Hold onto your meekness in the face of outbreaks of greed all around you. Don't want for much, but don't despair. Wait. Your inheritance will be coming in. Never mind that this old earth you're getting will be like a kicked-around Hacky Sack. Reverend Ike was up to something different.

We have no cathedral-scale shopping malls in Fairbanks, Alaska. People in need of the pinball experience of a mall shopping orgy must travel to Anchorage or the Lower 48. But we do have the postal service and, through it, a vast and interconnected array of goods available through catalogues. It is from these that I discover all my needs: custom-fitted neoprene waders in a variety of thicknesses, jaunty fishing hats, increasingly elaborate fishing vests. All the doodads and odds and ends to stuff in all those vest pockets. And rods and reels at breathtaking prices. It's in the pages of these catalogues I see I can still buy a newly made split-bamboo rod with two tips beginning at around fifteen hundred dollars.

What am I saying when I laugh and flip the catalogue in the trash and I just say "no"?

It's a harder question than it looks to be. It is the question of my life. How to have the beauty of the man in the boat—the long graceful casts, the rod catching the sunlight as the bamboo flexes, the absolute stillness of the lake—and have it honestly come by? For who would choose a world devoid of beauty—or of desire?

Our basement has taken to flooding on a semiannual basis. This last time, while I was down there moving everything that could be damaged up out of the water, I came upon the blue cardboard tube. My first fear was that I'd finished off the neglectful job somebody else started on this rod and it would now be ready for the Dumpster. But it was fine; it wasn't even damp. I carried it up out of the basement, took it out of its tube and bag, left the four sections sitting in

Kirke Woodward 1975

the corner of the living room for a few weeks, thinking that through merely looking at it I would get annoyed at the clutter and motivate myself to do something with the rod.

I took it to the Fly Shop, where a couple of state troopers were deep in a fly and tackle conference with Howie, the owner. I'd put the rod back in its tube and had been driving around with it stashed behind the seat of my truck for a week or so. Spring was coming in, and I guess I was beginning to get worked up about it. I pushed into the conversation, put my rod tube on the counter and began to open it up. The troopers starting guessing what I was going to show them.

"It's a bait casting rod."

"It's some sort of collapsible net or something."

"No, no," I said. "It's an old bamboo fly rod."

"Oh, yeah?" they said. Nobody in Alaska fishes with bamboo much, nobody I know but me, and at the time I was a committed doubter. A modern graphite rod, the kind Howie sells, so light, quick, and powerful, could almost be classified as a weapon. It will throw a line across a big Alaskan river; it will help you play in the most ornery of salmon right to your ankles.

I stood away from the pieces of the rod spread across the counter. I still wasn't sure I was willing to claim this thing as my own. A guy wants to watch himself in a place like the Fly Shop, in any sort of guy place—pool rooms, car lots, the high-up bleachers at ball games. To be secure in the company of men is, above all, never to appear foolish. Most likely the rod was junk, and how would I look thinking it could be anything else?

Well, Howie thought it wasn't so valuable that you'd be afraid to fish with it, though he wouldn't use it for anything bigger than trout and grayling. "Fix it up. You'll have some fun with it." I matched up the rusted guides with some brand-new chrome ones and left the shop.

In the Fly Shop, I had seen the promise of the bamboo fly rod's grace. I went back to my truck grinning like a dope in my self-satisfaction, picturing myself already casting this elegant old rod, and replaying Howie's advice on how to fix it, how to fish it. And then I stuck on his line about value. Exactly how valuable was it? And what did he mean by valuable anyway? One way to think of the value of my fly rod was in terms of the work and materials that went into it, the effort I would have to put into it to return it to use. Howie's certification, I decided, was not so much a measure of its monetary value, but of its usefulness, its potential for real fishing. I let myself relax a little because I found I truly wanted this fly rod. Having invested ten bucks or so in its restoration, I couldn't give it up now.

Then something worse happened. I considered the miracle of this rod. How I'd sat in my office so small that the only way to assemble a nine-foot fly rod was on the diagonal, and suddenly I was blessed with a nearly perfect, nearly fishable bamboo rod. I considered that if it came to me so innocently unannounced, then the world must be full of more of them. The attics, garages, and basements of America would be full of these wonderful rods, and some on-the-ball person could get them for free, or next to it. Yard sales, flea markets, estate auctions ought to be teeming with them. If this rod was a nine-foot, six-weight, maybe I should get ahold of a seven-and-a-half-foot, four- or five-weight, maybe an eight-footer, maybe a tiny three-weight. I wanted them all.

The people who came in my dad's store who left Reverend Ike's literature of promise and desire were poor, sometimes desperately poor. Whenever they got the chance, they would fill their homes with TV sets and furniture bought on easy terms, fill their yards with swing sets for the kids and fleets of broken cars. Like me, they had been caught wanting the things of the world, the near at hand, transient things, in place of what they needed, in place of beauty, in place of a truer kind of riches.

Clearly my rod was not worth thousands or even one thousand dollars. That, I thought, would be, in both Howie's mind and my own, too pricey to fall in a creek with. Because I could still fish with it, it had a truer value as a tool. But like certain baseball cards, glass telephone pole resistors, and other popular collectible junk, a fishing rod too can be made valuable because enough people get together and agree. I considered: I had driven it around in my unlocked truck. It could have been stolen. Yet by simply owning this bamboo fly rod, I might become the envy of my friends. The rod would be made useless, then. Valuable, but useless. But if it were less valuable—say in the hundreds—shouldn't I just give it back to Eric now?

Isn't it all just a trick of the mind? A trick that says having is enough? A seduction by the immediate, by what can be held in the hand, by what can be shown as proof? The rod in its current condition was useless, a bundle of sticks. What Howie saw in it was what it might be on the river someday, a fly rod put to its best use by fishing it.

Here's another thing I grew up hearing my mother say: "You don't need *that*," whatever *that* may have been—another model airplane, fishing lure, or odd article of clothing that struck my fancy. Hearing her words usually made me want whatever it was that much more. Years later, there would be a popping lure, yellow head with a white and green polka-dotted body, lying unused in a tray of my tackle box. If my mom recognized it and saw that it had never been in the water, she would say with a certain righteous pleasure, "And you had to have it."

Along the banks of my boyhood lake, dragonflies buzzed the air, indifferent to the distinction between water and land, indifferent to the limits of where a kid could and couldn't go. We called them snake doctors, though we rarely saw snakes and never thought at all about how dragonflies might have doctored any snaky diseases. Shiny, skinny and iridescent, scary, you didn't want one of them to get too close to you, to try to land on you. They darted and hung, sometimes singly, sometimes stacked in pairs. It was a long time later when I understood this was sex, sex flying through the air. But wasn't sex all over them? Wasn't it all over their snake patients, all tongue and slither, demanding that I acknowledge the current of desire running through them, through the world? Didn't they have an animal sense that I feared it? Desire could ruin you—look at the dragonfly carcasses scattered all around  the lake. It could change you too, like the snake that left its spent skin along the thwarts and oarlocks of the half-rotten rowboat.

This is what Reverend Ike taught us: to want everything. To justifiably want everything, unalloyed with the slightest trace of remorse for having more than our share, for having without needing. God's children don't have to wait to put on their simulated alligator shoes and drive around heaven all day. Jesus wants you to want everything now. This is not a new wrinkle in the old Protestant ethic wherein you got your just desserts through hard work, albeit allowing for a certain low cunning that helped you keep the equation simple: You worked hard, and that was good, and the stuff you accumulated was the proof of your goodness and to hell with everybody else. Jesus loves you, and he wants you to have it all.

My mom would have been right about the yellow-head plug with green polka-dots. I believe it is still rolling around in an old tackle box, still unused. And I know now I bought it to help fill every compartment in that tackle box. When I threw the box open beside the lake, I wanted it to look like a treasure chest of riches. But the plugs were all too big, the wrong colors, oddly shaped, bought for the promises of being hypnotically and irresistibly attractive. The yellow-head plug was especially egregious, so poorly designed that it could only catch a boy who was already caught by a frenzy of want.

Now I was in trouble. I went home from the Fly Shop and stared at the blue tube for a couple of more weeks, thought wishful thoughts about its contents, then slowly started stripping the rod for restoration. Before I could finish it, before I could actually fish with it, my wife and I went to Texas to see to her scholarly research. Fresh from Alaska, I saw Texas as a living monument to wanting everything. I understood this when we stood on a single floor of a department store where three acres or so of party dresses stretched out before us. The dresses were packed onto their racks so tightly that it would take the help of a salesperson to pull a few free to try on.

The fishing supply corner of Ched's, where I did my shopping as a boy, foresaw the Texas principle. In a ten-by-ten-foot area were cards full of spinners and spoons, jigs and dry flies sold in pairs inside tiny plastic boxes. The rocky rivers and weedy lakes of the southwest Virginia mountains would take all the equipment you could throw in them. Seeing all those lures, and picturing themselves caught up short

Kirke Woodward 1995

when the fish were on the bite, men stocked up their tackle boxes by the fistful.

Once, the company store in our town sold a few dozen dresses on a wholly different premise—that a woman could safely buy a dress and be fairly sure nobody else in town would have one like it. At least, there was the illusion of individuality. In that small corner of Ched's and in the shopping malls of Texas, though, something different took hold. Here were goods so thick they ought to be carried out in wheelbarrows. Such plenty encouraged a wild spirit of duplication. Everybody ought to have everything.

"You can only fish with one at a time" was what my mother said. She had never seen Fuzzy Elmore hunting the largemouth bass. Fuzzy Elmore had a sheaf of identical Shakespeare Wonder Rods arrayed in the stern of his boat, each set up with a different lure, and I saw that here was another principle: Be prepared for all contingencies.

I went to a couple of Texas-sized flea markets, read the want ads, went to likely looking estate sales and antique auctions. There I saw confirmed what I already believed, that people are like locusts. Once provoked, they will consume everything in sight—cups with broken handles, dying potted plants, worn shoes that don't really fit—with no thought as to what good any of it might finally do them. At one flea market, my wife bought some cowboy boots; I bought a racquet-ball racket. I found no bamboo fly rods, and not finding them seemed to only heighten my wanting. I had to have more.

One time a river got the best of me. Trying to cross over in thigh-deep water to a hole where I was sure a big fish was waiting for me, I felt the force of the river, saw it climbing up my legs as I hesitated.

16

With two good steps, I could be in the place I wanted. I took a step and I found myself knocked over by the current, carried maybe a hundred, a hundred fifty feet downriver only to pop out in an eddy where I couldn't find the bottom. I got swept away by wishes too big for me, too strong. Sitting on the bank, chastened and wet, I let my body tell me what it knew. I'd almost drowned.

I went to the fly-fishing store in Austin, a small, unassuming place located upstairs from the High Times Tea Room and Brain Gym. A Range Rover was parked outside, and inside the store, its owner and his pal were pricing their first-ever fly outfits. The guy running the store was loading them up with the most expensive gear he had to offer, and they weren't flinching. I knew what would happen to all that gear, and the salesman probably did too. These two middle-aged guys' idea of fishing up to this moment was cruising a reservoir, flipping lures out of an overpowered, sparkle-painted bass boat. They would never put in the time to learn fly-fishing, and being too vain to fish badly in public, they'd soon ditch their fancy new gear in a closet.

When I got my chance, I asked the guy where I might look for older bamboo rods. He said they didn't deal in bamboo rods. I told him about my own rod and my start on its restoration.

"Yeah, well, that's a production rod. I see a couple of those a month. They're kind of heavy and slow."

"Oh," I said. "I was hoping to find a smaller rod that'd take a lighter line."

"So is everybody," he told me. And he gave me a newsletter full of bamboo rods in various states of repair and disrepair, all for sale.

Now I knew. I knew "production rod" was a mild insult in the world of bamboo rods. It was like owning a Ford or Chevrolet in the company of people who drove Jaguars. And I knew that the guy who'd told my colleague the rod was worthless also was right in his way. A Shakespeare rod like mine in excellent shape was worth about what I would have put into the restoration: new guides, wraps, varnish, and time—provided my time were worth about a dollar an hour. The only way it would be worth having was to fix it up, take it to the river and put it to use.

I also knew I lived in a world where everybody seemed to have already decided what everything was worth. Before I had ever thought of wanting an old bamboo rod for myself, somebody out there had anticipated my want and set up a little newsletter to accommodate me. A good old bamboo fly rod costs just what you would imagine, in the hundreds and even the thousands of dollars. And anybody who grew up in a family that fished such rods would know their worth as well. They were expensive then; they're expensive now.

I cherish certain prejudices about fly-fishing. One is that fly-fishers are better people all around—more inclined to put their fish back in the river, less inclined to leave their litter on the banks. Your better fishing people are fly-fishers. Doesn't that notion come from the old four-porthole Buick crowd, though? Fly-fishers are better people simply because they're drawn from a better class of people, a more monied class?

Could it be that a fly-fisher studies the natural world, the world of fish and the bugs they eat, the places they live and cannot live until it must become clear to him that he's a part of it all, part of great nature too? I want to believe this. Fish are greedy rascals, as greedy as people. Fear of getting eaten is all that keeps their greed in check. Each fish we catch is a fish that has allowed its greed to overcome its sense of caution.

Like all the rest of America, I have been successfully conditioned to want everything. But thanks to my mother and father, I have been conditioned more strongly in the ways of cheapness. My basement is filled with the by-products of greed and cheapness—cardboard boxes the computer came in, the stereo came in; trash bags filled with accumulated foam peanuts; scrap lumber; bins of nuts, bolts, and screws, many picked up out of the roadway. I can't throw them away because, as Mom says, "Better to have it and not need it than to need it and not have it." Keeping this junk around has one good end: it triggers momentary attacks of revulsion at having so much stuff. I cannot throw it away, but just looking at it wears me out. I give up on wanting more.

Out fishing for trout, I find the river full of dead king salmon. These swam—and have consumed themselves in the swimming— a couple of hundred river miles to get here. They have changed from silver-bright to a deep glowing red to a mottled and tattered dun, their flesh rotting off them even as they lived. Their carcasses lie on the banks, ride in the eddies, jam between river rocks like water-logged tree limbs. They've done what they came here to do.

I could never drop two thousand dollars in a day on fishing tackle like the two rich Range Roving Texans. What, though, is so bad about that? There are worse things to spend money on. And since they'll most likely never wind up crowding my favorite fishing holes, why should I care? Sometime up the road, their mint-condition late-twentieth-century equipment will be a bargain to be found in another collectors' newsletter.

This cheapness is not a virtue. It's niggling and dangerous and causes a person to drive on bald tires, to go too long between oil changes and delay painting the house until it needs scraping and a new undercoat too. It causes me to buy things I don't particularly need because they are on sale and I cannot resist this fraudulent way of saving. In this way I prove I am as dumb as a fish. We all are. We always have been.

And yet there is this to be said about my wanting. It is a good, necessary thing. A thing I'm afraid no fish can understand. Beauty, grace, desire—elements of the human animal's world—what is life without them? I am thinking of a grayling, oblivious to its wonder-working ways, holding in the current where Cripple Creek dumps into the Chatanika River. Moving out into the faster water to take a fly, it is a fish living its fishy life.

Caught and in my hand, the fish is a miracle of calico blue with spotted circles down its sides. Sunlight shakes rainbowed iridescence from its scales. Its long dorsal fin trails like a pennant, and in its other fins, rays of turquoise and orange shoot through the black.

A cast of my bamboo rod has directed me to this place, this moment, this fish. And I find that it is not in the having but in the using of this rod that I have found a way to live with my wanting. Catching this grayling has let me see again the beauty in the world; it has done me some good. I let the fish slip back into the water and it settles to the bottom, near my feet, confused and worn out. In a few minutes it will be back in the water column again, feeding. I will move on up the river, casting under the cut banks, into the eddies, and behind the sweepers. To be out on the river is enough.

saying as I go,
"What the hell,
it works."

THE AGE OF IMPERFECTION

In the middle of the winter, between midnight and one-thirty in the morning, I have gone to my basement, taken up my brush and varnish, and done a piss-poor job of refinishing my bamboo fly rod. It's not just the varnish. In fact, the varnish itself comes out looking fairly good. It's the whole shebang, everything rolled into one, every error I made in wrapping the rod that is now brought to my attention as I apply the varnish and the brush draws my eye to each bit of stubble sticking out between the wraps, each fuzzy fray, every uneven spacing within the thread, to the wobbly alignments of the decorative signature wraps near the butt.

I recognize even as I am making this mess that I am tired, that midnight is a ridiculous hour to set out upon such a tedious task. I recognize, as I keep applying the varnish over one mistake after another, that I am only compounding my errors. I keep working, and as

I do I meditate on myself and on my age and how these times and I have conspired to make my fishing rod into a metaphor for so many things so imperfectly done.

Here is what I want to say about imperfection: You would think that its mirror opposite, perfection, could be managed easily enough, at least on the small scale of a single fishing rod. How much could there be to it? That there are books on the subject of bamboo rod restoration should surprise no one. These days, there are helpful books on every subject. But the simple knowledge is not the issue. It is the goal of making one perfect thing accompanied by my notion that if I could get just one small spot in my disordered life nailed down neatly and precisely, then I would at least feel I had a shot at some modicum of control over the rest of it.

There is a big, almost empty museum in Austin, Texas, filled with a few dinosaur bones and lots of guns. The guns are arrayed in chronological order in glass cases around the perimeter of one room. I've never cared much about guns, but since it didn't take me very long to look at the few bones, I took my time on the guns. You could say there was a certain curve of expectation played out there. In the beginning of their development, guns were roughly made, poorly functional things looking as likely to blow up in your face as to shoot your intended target. Nowadays there are functional factory-machined guns. If you are drawn to an aesthetic of ugliness, and if you believe that a mechanism designed to do an ugly job—for what other jobs might an Uzi do?—ought to have a matching aesthetic appeal, then modern guns have arrived at a companionable level of accomplishment.

In between ancient guns and modern guns were some guns I would have to call beautiful. Many of these were made in Renaissance Italy, and the source of their beauty was the crafted metal work that covered the barrels, the trigger guards, even the hammers with fili-greed, rococo swirls. My friend Jeff, a blacksmith and saddle maker, will tell you that a design with spare, clean lines is harder to pull off than a fancy one. You can hide a world of mistakes in ornamentation. But as I said, I had plenty of time to spend in the museum, and I looked at the guns with my most persnickety eye. I could detect no goofs.

I turned my thoughts to my bamboo rod back home in Alaska, left behind and then only halfway toward restoration. I was thinking about the aesthetics of ordinary things, about the expectations we bring to houses and cars and fishing rods, whether we're conscious of them or not. These might be emblems of the brief prospect of the perfect within our imperfect world. Witness the boy who has poured his soul into his car, meticulously maintained and parked diagonally through three spaces at the most distant edge of the asphalt apron surrounding the supermarket where he bags groceries.

You poor kid, I could tell him, the world with its loose gravel and careless drivers and slushy road salt is waiting to ambush you around every corner. I have had my affair with the car and know once the driver's seat grows as comfortable to slip into as a broken-in shoe, the inevitable decay of body, frame, and engine cannot be too long in coming. Cars are made to wear out, to be disposed of. It wasn't always this way.

I've heard that quilters used to introduce mistakes into their quilts on purpose, a forced humility. For the perfect quilt would be a brassy accomplishment, a kind of homespun hubris. Who were these quilters, I always wanted to know, who could come so close to perfection that they saw the need to create mistakes? Or was the purposeful mistake an admission of a truer knowledge of how the world works? No matter how beautiful a quilt might be to begin with, its function was to cover a bed where it would be rolled upon and sweated into and kicked off onto the floor, where the sick child home from school might spill his tomato soup on it, might throw up on it, or worse. The washings alone would fade and wear the cloth. Better to start it back down its road to rags yourself, better not make it so perfect as to tempt somebody to store it away from its intended use.

I come from a family where life is a forced march through mistakes. My mother is an expert at turning away compliments in just this way. Anybody foolish enough to admire one of her aprons or dresses or small watercolor paintings will only be made to scrutinize all the mistakes anybody could plainly see if only they took time to look. Thanks to her lesson, I cultivated my own self-critical eye, an eye that must willfully light on every imperfection until I have grown to be a storehouse of knowledge, a compilation of all my varied and multiplied errors. Anything I write can only be an accumulation of clumsily chosen words, sentences that are overlong, too short, never exactly what I mean. Sentences that, try as I might, I cannot make better.

There is another way of looking at this problem, a way

out of the trap of perpetual shortcomings and disappointments, which is to take up my poorly finished fly rod and take it fishing, saying as I go, "What the hell, it works." It does; it works as well as a fifty-something, modestly priced fly rod can work. And it would work better still if I were more disciplined in my casting, less leisurely in my back cast, more resistant to the temptation to carry my delivery too far forward. When I do my part, the rod does pretty well.

Probably this rod was made for Shakespeare in the South Bend Bait Company factory. Most Shakespeare rods of its era were. And it was made by men and women who went to work every day with their dinner buckets, took up their tools, and built fly rods. When I look at it this way, my rod seems a small wonder to me. There is a level of precision in its manufacture that would take me, or anybody in my spot who took a notion to learn the craft of building bamboo fishing rods from scratch, years to master. I am sure it took the people at the South Bend factory some time to achieve their particular skills too. I respect that. But I guess I am more respectful of their daily devotion to work that must be done with constant attention and care if it is to be done at all. My old rod still has snug ferrules, clean straight sticks of planed, tapered bamboo glued tightly together and meant to stay that way. To make such rods day in and day out would require an allegiance to the product even if you didn't have an in-kling of where it might wind up, of its meliorative uses in our world. And it would require a similar assumption about the person who would come to own it. Maker and owner would share the ideal of some beautiful, perfect thing, or at least the prospect of a perfectible thing and maybe a perfectible world to go with it.

■ 27

One time a friend of mine hollered at me, "You're a closet Platonist!" The subject was aspects of beautiful women. "Me?" I said, sounding a little bit like Saint Peter. But I will say again, I have no special desire to go with Plato into his musty cave. To do so is to acknowledge that perfection is not for this earth. To do so is to surrender myself up to some cosmic otherness. Plato says we should try for perfection always, strive to achieve it through the manufacture of the lowest table, chair, or fishing pole with the hope of someday perfecting the form. By doing so we have ratcheted our way from ash wood to bamboo to fiberglass to graphite. But the true fly rod—the kind the gods surely cast with perfect grace, always with the right fly, always provoking a strike—is not for us to know, not for this life.

Through thinking of the perfect fly rod, I might free myself from the itchy desires of this earth. But why would I want to? Democritis tells us atoms once fell like rain, in perfect parallel paths. Nothing else happened for a long time until one day an atom swerved and hit a neighbor atom. From that happy accident, a chain reaction of crashes and collisions, atoms sticking together and sheering apart, there came to be a universe, a world, plants, animals, people, and fish. I see myself as a walking sack of accidents, a happenstantial combination of genetic matches, a few of them mistakes. Yet I'm happy to be here, in the world of the nickel curveball, Billie Holiday, and Jackson Pollack, wouldn't have it any other way.

Imperfection is the wonder of this world, the door we might walk through to find what is possible, what is new. In this way I find myself standing on a gravel bar looking through my fly box for some pattern I have not tried on these reluctant silver salmon. Maybe if the fish were fresher, if I had come a week or so earlier, I would have better luck. Maybe. But I look for another fly, which probably won't do the trick since all Pacific salmon flies are pretty much the same—big, bright, garish, and weighted to cast like rocks. As I do, I hear a honking conversation in the sky and look up to see a flock of twenty or so birds coming over the trees toward me. At first I think they're geese, but as they cross overhead I can see from their amazing necks and white bodies that they're trumpeter swans. Another smaller flight comes behind them, these too caught up in whatever discussions they have of wind speed and distance and good stopping places for the night. I have heard the small lakes around the Alaskan Interior are popular resting places with these birds, that it's possible to come out at sunrise and see hundreds settled on the water. I've not seen that sight yet, but it is a promised accidental encounter that makes fishing more than catching fish.

Just now, as I look down at my feet, a fresh fly in one hand and the tip of my leader in the other, I see five silver salmon, already growing bright red, their heads growing blacker, swimming up and over the gravel bar a few inches from my feet. By the time I secure my knot and cast, I will have missed them. It won't matter. I have had my chances all day with the small schools of two to six fish passing up the river. I've put my varied flies right in their faces, and they've brushed by them. Right at their spawning grounds, and late in their run, they are set for one thing only. I have to admire their narrow purpose and their indifference to mine.

All this I have witnessed through the miracle of my bad luck, of being on the river at the wrong time, or having the wrong flies, or choosing the wrong moment to tie a different pattern on my leader. All this is a triumph of accident, of imperfection.

In Plato's heaven, there would be nothing to do all day. Everything would already be known; everything would already be done; whatever was going to happen would have already happened. Our vague yearnings for a beautiful world would be satisfied. The perfect fishing hole we always thought was out there somewhere would be right before our very eyes. Fish, like L'il Abner's Schmoos, would gladly surrender themselves up to us. And would we gratefully put them back in the river? Or would we eat them, sure in our knowledge that they wanted to be eaten all along? Either way, fishing could only quickly grow tiresome.

Well now, I think, before I get too far along in my celebration of randomness, a fly rod might be so poorly made that it would be no kind of fishing rod at all, but a bundle of sticks and thread and bits of metal. My own desk covered with books and papers and feathers, hooks, and stray bits of fur can become a triumph of the accidental, a work of art in the style of that random constructionist Kurt Schwitters until I need to find my checkbook. Which is to say that nobody I know has completely succeeded in letting go of order, which is to say the ideal of perfection. Some rods cast better than others; some people cast better than others too. And anybody who fishes very much has a pretty good idea of what *better* is.

It kept striking me as funny, all these insubstantial symbols of the seasons strewn about the landscape. I've seen maple leaves no bit of *pin pleures if cause and chyche and a soundes edge that I'm days wore, that shapes after, but I am thopt of them a shape.*

I used to paint houses with a bunch of guys who would stand back from a job and declare, "It'll pass." You might think that a low standard unless you saw the work of these painters who could not abide the spray gun or roller, who only held with the sash tool and brush. Passing was their only standard, and I learned it one step at a time, beginning with cleaning my brush until I got it right. Outside the job before them, their lives were shot full of chaos. Standing on the edge of their world as a part-timer college kid, even I could see that. In the disorder of dissolving marriages, bad debts, broken cars, or newer ones on the verge of going back to the bank and weekend-long boozing sprees, they often missed days of work or came in looking too hungover to manage their jobs. But once they had their tools in hand, they could get through the day. A brush in the hand steadied their shakes.

When casting a fly, the only thing to think about is casting a fly. When restoring a fly rod, the best thing to think about is just that series of tasks. There are tricks, and some tricks are learned only the hard way: when to cut the thread with a razor blade, when to burn it with a flame, when to thin the lacquer and how much. Some jobs just have to be redone until they will pass. The materials of the mechanical age are forgiving; it's almost as if a process of wear and replacement is expected. After a full summer of fishing with my bamboo rod, of finding out its possibilities and its limits, I am now headed back to the basement to begin again, to strip the rod of its wraps and guides and varnish, to put it all back together again.

The TV set preaches "More and newer." Sitting exposed to its electron wind, I find the message hard to resist. The world is chock-full of goods; we're tempted to scoop them up with an end-loader, haul them home, and sit on our treasures. When they begin to fade, as surely they must since it's programmed into their design and manufacture, then we have to go out and get more.

I wonder if there isn't another way. In repairing this rod, in fishing with it, I have to ask myself if I'm learning anything aside from narrow, antique skills. Whether the well-made rod, the well-placed cast serve me in the chaotic world. A trip to the river is a series of actions and choices. One of my painter friends, the one who taught me the most, fell out of a fishing boat while drunk and drowned. I went back to college after advancing my skills to the level of painting a kitchen with enamel. I think I seek a means, a method, but not an end. A trip to the river is a series of actions and choices. Which fly? Where to cast? How best to reach the spot I'm aiming for? Some days I don't catch a thing, some days I catch quite a few. Fly-fishing takes a mulish patience, a recognition of limits, a willingness to put up with mistakes, take them in, learn from them. On the river, the world is neither perfect nor broken, but always fixable, adjustable, always ripe for restoration. It's a good place for a bamboo fly rod.

But what
is it
good for?

USEFUL TOOLS

It seems like every Sunday there's a Sears sale flier stuck in the newspaper. On the back page, past the ads for polyester clothing, kitchen appliances, and snow tires come the Craftsman tools. There are always a few specialty tools, vise-grips, torque wrenches and such, with their own individual pictures. But the highlight of the tool section is a big half-page picture offering richly arrayed complete Craftsman tool sets. Ranks of standard sockets, metric sockets, deep-welled sockets, foam-lined spark plug sockets stand ready to serve me. Behind the sockets are the various socket driving devices—swivel-headed, ratcheted, screwdriver style, shorty. Fanned sets of screwdrivers both flat-blade and Phillips, Allen keys, open-end and box wrenches, standard and metric, are offered as inviting side attractions. All these stout tools parade in front of a multidrawered tool box, promising a lifetime warranty of usefulness, of jobs well done.

They're good tools. A good tool invites you to take it up. I felt the urge in an art supply store while looking at a cabinet of woodworking tools, sharp gouges with balled wooden handles. A sign warned me they were sharp, to ask a salesperson for assistance. And while I knew this sign was true, that these tools would quickly find their way into the soft flesh of my hands, I wanted to take them up and handle them. Seeing them, I believed I could carve.

A good tool is beautiful to work with, though not necessarily beautiful to look at. I think I see its beauty by imagining its use. The bamboo fly rod when broken down is a clumsy collection of sticks. Put together, it's a gangly thing threatening to poke an eye out, or to run itself against a tree trunk or topple underfoot and get broken. The only place it makes sense, the only place it can do its work is on the open space of a river.

A good tool can often be a simple thing. Remember the six basic machines from General Science class? The wedge, the lever, the wheel and axle, the pulley, the incline plane, the screw. Only I don't think of any of these as machines at all. I hold with Scott Russell Sanders's idea that a tool is used by hand, which is to say it has few moving parts and no motor. An Eskimo harpoon is such a tool, a good tool, elegant in its simplicity. Its toggled head represents a breakthrough in human ingenuity. When such a harpoon strikes an animal, the head comes free of the shaft and swivels onto its side, becoming a barb that's hard to pull out.

A harpoon, a claw hammer, an axe, a bicycle spoke wrench, even a Sears Craftsman socket set—these are the kinds of tools I like. I don't trust myself around machinery; I cut the little wood we use in our inefficient stove with an axe and handsaw, then split it with a maul. The advantage to these tools is that they allow me to work at my easy pace, not the pace of a machine. They let me work within my limited human strength. When I find myself jumping on the handle of a lug wrench because my truck has come back from the shop with its wheels put on with an air gun, I see how readily a machine seizes the advantage over a human.

I'm not sure what sort of tool a fly rod is. A long, long lever maybe, something like the throwing boards that both Eskimos and Greeks and who-knows-who else devised to throw spears farther. Except a fly rod transfers its force to a flexible line, not a rigid shaft. A fly rod delivers its force at its tip-top where it drives the line along forward and back—greater force equals more line over a longer distance. The line itself rolls that power down its length until the nearly weightless leader and fly take what little energy is left and float out softly over the water. A well-executed cast looks so elegant, so simple. It pretty much is, which is why, while people keep trying to make fly rods out of different materials, the idea of the rod has remained the same.

Until graphite came along, the best fly rods were still made from Tonkin cane, a kind of bamboo, seasoned and split and planed and glued together. Graphite rods are made from cloth of graphite fiber rolled onto steel mandrels and cooked. They're just hollow fibrous tubes with remarkable qualities of strength and flexibility. A graphite rod weighs less than one made of bamboo, will cast a fly farther, and requires less care and attention. Fishing with bamboo requires a contrary attitude.

In a secondhand store I came upon a whole bin of fine wooden tennis racquets. I looked on their laminated bows and shafts, the varied colors and textures of the wood, which marries perfectly with a leather grip. Such wonderful craftsmanship, and I could have had any of them—Wilson Kramer, T. A. Davis, the racquets I had coveted in my youth—for a couple of bucks. Philosophers have been trying for ages to connect the beautiful and the good, and from time to time so do we all. There's some expectation of that whenever we take up any tool. Here is a usefulness created out of the countless trials and errors that took us from a fist-shaped rock to a framing hammer.

My dad once got a metal-handled framing hammer as a premium in a carton of bubblegum sent to his store. The hammer looked like a Stanley, but it wasn't. He gave it to a pal of his who was a sometime carpenter. That carpenter was carrying it home when an old jackleg saw it and took a shine to it. He was the kind of hillbilly whose idea of a good-looking car was a pink and white Ford Fairlane. Nobody in our town owned one of those new all-metal hammers, which is why he had to have it and paid ten dollars for the gimme hammer. The first time he used it to drive a few nails, the head folded right over.

Last summer I started taking out a good graphite rod, five-weight, and my six-weight bamboo rod when I went for grayling. I was thinking about that bargain bin of tennis racquets and the gimme hammer, about the beautiful and the good and how often we want them to be the same thing and how rarely they are. I'd start out with my bamboo rod, standing the other in some bushes up on the bank. I'd work

some line out and begin to false cast, then lay my dry fly on the water. It made me feel like a kid playing catch with my friends, throwing a baseball back and forth in an easy rhythm while we talked away the small worries of our kid lives.

What material could be more wondrous than wood? I ask, knowing that strictly speaking bamboo is a kind of grass. But it has the qualities I appreciate in wood. From a distance, my rod is a dark honey blond. Up close, you can see the variation in the fibers from those that are almost black to lighter ones to the bursts of near white where the nodes have been planed out of the cane. Anything made of wood invites you in to its design, draws the eye to the play of shapes within a shape.

Graphite is just what color you would expect, the color of pencil lead, though nowadays most graphite rods are coated with a wrap of cooked-on cellophane, browns or greens mostly. Blue is common, and I have even heard of purple. If I hold the rod up to the light I can see a kind of Space Age effect, ring upon ring running through the length of the rod telling of the heat that made it. I know this rod; I built it from the blank. The brown looked like a Baptist deacon's Sunday suit, so I wrapped it in orange tipped in powder blue. There is something of the hillbilly's two-tone Fairlane in that rod, of the jackleg hillbilly in me. I'm pulled to newfangledness yet resist it at the same time.

I want to resist the graphite fly rod on account of its nylon wrapping thread, its epoxy finishing coat, its disconnectedness from the natural world. There's a kind of hubris in the materials, promising to last the ages, designed to be eternally discarded. A graphite rod tip will snap off against a tree trunk just like bamboo, but then what have you got? And what do you do with it?

Last summer I would find myself reaching for the graphite rod, especially if the fish weren't rising to dry flies. Though it carried a lighter line, it would throw it farther, throw a weighted nymph or a woolly bugger almost as well as a dry fly. Maybe because there is less wobble out at the rod tip, it throws a straighter, cleaner line. There's no denying it's the better tool.

Down at the Chowder House, they have a whole variety of bamboo fishing rods on display. The Chowder House does serve chowder, but it's a quiche and salad, sandwich, real-estate-dealers-meet-for-lunch kind of place. The rods are part of a decorating scheme that includes fish swimming on the curtains and on the napkins, walls covered by old calendar prints of fish and fishermen coming to terms. I'm not sure I'm in favor of turning fishing rods into decor, turning fishing into background. In the middle of the room, for example, there's a giant bamboo casting rod strung up along the ceiling, some heavy line coming off the reel to where it's attached to a metal cutout of a fish. I look at this bit of self-satisfied cleverness and think about what such a rod might be good for if left in a boat where it belonged.

The fly rods themselves are held prisoners in a clear Plexiglas rack, made something like a multistory gun rack. Each rod is broken down into its sections and tied down to the rack by those plastic wire ties sold at car parts stores. From the looks of them, some of these rods were well used but are still fishable with a little work. Some have probably been ruined; they've outlasted their usefulness.

I wonder what could be worse. When a fly rod is no longer a fly rod, it's a bunch of funny-looking sticks. I say this as a person who saves all kinds of junk—screws, nuts, bolts, bits of wire and rope—because they might eventually serve some yet to be imagined purpose. Taken together, they have a kind of potential energy. An ex–fly rod doesn't as long as it's caught up in representing what it used to be.

I wonder what makes people want to hang tools on the walls of restaurants in the first place. Crosscut saws and double-bit axes are popular, spades and rakes and rusty hoes. Those people mean well, I think. They mean to say something about such tools and the people who used them. *Those were the days, that was work,* I am supposed to be thinking to myself as I feed my face. As if the choices we have made to walk away from such implements weren't just that—a series of choices that made us warm, dry, and comfortable eating food we didn't even have to cook ourselves. It's a pretty good life, but we would rather wallow. In days gone by, there were men of gold, then of silver, then bronze; but we are men of tin. We don't even wash our own dishes. As if breaking a sweat were a gesture of moral superiority.

I don't think that's all of it. Nobody with a sense of history would want to go back to hard labor, child labor, diseases, discomfort, tedium, and early death. Nobody could say suffering made those old folks better. There's the suggestion, though, of life as straight and purposeful as a hickory hoe handle, as clear as the difference between a vegetable and a weed. It has its appeal: a wish for fewer moving parts, a wish for more tools and fewer machines.

In this way I can catch myself nostalgic for what never was, a world with fewer complications, fewer webs of entanglement, a world more within my grasp. Yet fly-fishing, particularly fly-fishing with a bamboo rod older than I am, is a willful compounding of complexity. Sometimes I think a fly rod may be no kind of tool at all. Wasn't the General Science expectation of the six simple machines that each reduce the amount of effort required to get a job done? If it's fish you want, the mocking old cartoons are right. More often than not, the kid with the willow branch, worms, and bobber beats the fly fisherman with his vest full of gadgets.

Some days a fly rod might just make fishing harder. Down on Dismal Creek, walled in by laurel thicket on both banks, with only slick limestone rocks to stand on, I saw how far I have to go in my study of side-arm, backhand, and curve casts. I thought about the word "presentation," what it meant to me and what it meant to a brook trout holding in low, clear water. I've traded the possibility of success simply come by for something more complex and more open to failure: the delicate leader, the fly that alludes to life but isn't, the tricky casting required to get the whole apparatus out there. It can be a beautiful undertaking.

But what is it good for? I ask myself, not because there are days when fly-fishing seems like a bad use of a pretty good tool. A fly rod just helps me put a good fly up a tree beyond my reach. On the days

I've used my rod better, made crisp casts, caught beautiful fish and most often released them, what good has it done me?

My friends who don't fish wonder how fishing could be a worthwhile undertaking. I've spent another day inflicting pain and terror on some of Great Nature's dumber creatures. And which is worse, putting them back or eating them? I admit I cannot answer these questions except to say, so do we all. We move through our comfortable lives with central heat and packaged food, having bent nature to our shape as we pleased. Yet if our daily misuse of nature is coy and disingenuous, my recognition of the cruelty built into fishing is no better. Does it help to say I think about it, that I wonder what sort of mechanism this world is and what part I play in its vast system of cogs and wheels?

I went out on the Chatanika in the late fall, not sure how far upriver to go since the fish drop down as it gets colder, looking for warm holes to spend the winter. When I got off the road, I passed the camp of some moose hunters and saw where the tracks of their four-wheelers led to the river and crossed in the tail of a long shallow pool. I would spend most of my time fishing that long hole without any success, thinking maybe I was too late in coming to this spot, thinking about this, that, and the other as well. Before that day was out, I found the end of a short story I had been working on, although I didn't know I was looking for it. I thought that story was done. Suddenly, standing in the middle of the river, I knew it wasn't and knew what it needed. The sentences slid right out onto my notebook. Then I looked at the river and into my fly box and thought of the Elk Hair Caddis.

I kept two of the bigger fish for dinner, and when I cut them open they were both full of bees. That was the fall of 1994 after the summer when, if we told time like they did in the old days, we would have called it the summer everybody got stung by bees. Two nests hung out over the water; I saw them now. As the bees died off going into winter, they fell to the fish waiting below them. My wife and I ate the fish. Through the winter I would work up some flies on a bee pattern. I would rewrite my short story and see that it worked better.

What was that day good for? Why did finding an end to my short story require my presence on the river? And what was this luck but putting a good tool to an unintended use? I ask as a past expert at putting tools to unintended uses, screwdrivers for pry bars and chisels, knife blades for screwdrivers, anything within reach for a hammer. I ruined some tools that way, yet my tying bench is full of straightened paper clips, knotted rubber bands, dissecting needles, scalpels, and bits of razor blade lashed into skinny dowels— a collection of small, necessary inventions.

I ask because I doubt anything ever coming of our wished-for marriage of the beautiful and the good. I ask because I keep looking just the same. I take up the bamboo fly rod and ask. And then I take up the graphite rod and ask again. I use them both to try to catch fish, but end up just as often catching other odd things that come my way. I consider the good and not-so-good uses of any tool, our intentions when we take tools up, and the results we get. I consider the way a tool teaches us how to love our work and how it can come to make itself more valuable than its few simple parts.

"It's going to be slow," he told me

ON HIS SLOWNESS

When I started shoveling, I thought I could get all that snow up in an hour. Soon it would be two hours, and I was not finished yet. Why was this? Why have I always thought I should be able to do everything I do faster: run faster, ski faster, even read and write faster? I picture myself as a boy, a first or second grader, running down the hill in front of our house with my friends Tim Nowlin and Alfred Martin. They're running off and leaving me, not out of some fit of childhood meanness, but because I cannot keep up. Even at that age, I was what I would become, a wobbly bag of bones, nothing but knees and elbows and big feet slapping the pavement. I am slow.

Unconsciously connecting with this long-recognized truth, I started to sing "On Top of Old Smokey" as I shoveled: "On top of old Smokey / All covered with snow . . ." I tried to remember, was it snow or smoke? Snow seemed more appropriate on this day, so snow is how I sang it. "I lost my true love / For courting too slow." How, I wondered, could anybody possibly court too slow? Sex and love both seem to me to be studies in the arts of delay and anticipation. Every Saturday night, my high school girlfriend and I played at this game. Parked out some muddy road to nowhere, we explored the varieties of kissing until our lips were numb. We went on to cautious probes through each other's clothing, then to opening buttons and snaps. The chill air in the car on suddenly bare flesh. The hoped-for and never-quite-arrived-at climactic moment. This is what we were learning, the pleasures found in opening the world out slowly, slowly. The pleasures found in the space of waiting.

Fishing is like that for me, but not necessarily for everybody. I took Chris, my wife's nephew, fishing. It turned out he hadn't done much fishing, and like most people who haven't, he wanted his fish and he wanted them now. It was already raining when we drove up, and I left all the reels in a canvas bag at home. By the time I got back to the riverbank with them the water was rising and carrying bits of debris. Within a couple of hours it was high, fast, and muddy. I made my way from dry flies to nymphs to streamers. The fish went down and stayed there. In a long day in the rain, I got a couple of fish on with my darkest streamers, but I didn't land either one. Chris didn't get near a fish. We got skunked.

It happens; it's part of fishing's cosmic wheel. Sometimes I go out there and look like a genius. Every cast seems perfect, every placement provokes a fish, every fly I try seems to produce. Playing a fish

turns into another chore; I'm a little relieved when one slips the hook. I find myself using those off-the-wall flies I tied up one day just to try a different pattern. I'm looking to find the fly that *won't* work.

And sometimes I look like an idiot. I hang up my back cast high in a tree; I overshoot my cast into the brush on the far bank and stand there looking at my dangling fly in a branch across a stretch of current too deep or too swift to wade. What's there to do but try to whip my rod around with the vague hope my line will work loose until I give up and break off? No accounting of my life as a fisherman would be completely honest without admitting to all the above moments, good and bad. While they may demonstrate why I prefer to fish alone, I've come to accept them as the balled-up elements of who I am.

Gradually I've come to see acceptance itself as an aspect of my slowness, an attitude that says, *Take it easy, this is how the world goes, this is how you are one part of it.* A deep current runs through my bones, the essential truth of slowness. With this knowledge, I wish I could go back to stand by my high school track coach as he watched me flail

around the football field and could not understand why I was not the quarter miler of his dreams. Or the college coach who mistook me for a high hurdler. I could tell them to forget it.

It has its advantages, my slowness. An irate student comes into my office and harangues me about her grade. Hours later I consider that her words have been peppered with insults. Of course, I'm angry now too, but the student is safely out of sight. By the time I see her again I will have slowly calmed down. When I was young I could fall in love before I ever figured out what it was that hit me. By the time I did, it  was too late; I'd missed the boat. I stayed out of mischief for a while that way. I went fishing a lot where I found I could stand for hours in cold creek water up to the knees of my wet blue jeans, casting what seems like thousands of times in a day to fish that might not have even been down there. Which is how slowness teaches acceptance. Most of the time in fishing, nothing happens. You just wait. It took me a long time to learn that you are supposed to wait, and I still forget that lesson from time to time.

Which is to say when the bamboo fly rod came into my hands, it seemed like it was made just for me. I said to Howie at the Fly Shop as he advised me on how to fix it up, "It's going to be slow, isn't it?"

"It's going to be slow," he told me with maybe a shade of regret in his voice. It wasn't like I was getting the hard news after my kid's first IQ test. Having long since accepted my own slowness, I saw my perfect match.

The first fly-fishing outfit I owned was a Garcia rod and a heavy spring-retrieval reel. I had seen a guy fishing with such a combination, and not having seen any other fly fishermen up close, I thought this was the reel to have. I ordered the rod out of a wholesale catalogue catering to business people. Among the odd assortment of musical instruments and transits, tasteless jewelry, and adding machines, I came upon a fly rod. Not knowing where else to look, I ordered it. When it arrived at the end of winter, it was nine and a half feet long and thick as my thumb—a lot of rod for bluegill, which is what I mostly caught.

And it was slow. I didn't know; I couldn't know. For years it was my only rod. It took a long time for me to find the feel of casting, having only the illustrations in a Boy Scout merit badge book to help me. It took me just as long to learn the feel of the clutch in our Chevrolet. In both cases, it was because I was clumsy as well as slow. Or maybe slow because I was simply clumsy. Often they go together. But I did learn the fly rod. Once I felt its rhythm and learned to wait for the back cast, learned to wait for the fly resting on the lake, learned to wait until just about dark when the serious fish got interested, I knew I'd never tire of it.

When I am fishing, time becomes elastic. My wife and I have an understanding. I fish while she sits on the bank in her foldout chair, reads a book, and waits. How long to wait is always a matter for negotiation. There is never enough time to be on a river once we have arrived. My own sense of time is governed by each cast and its drift, by each hole, no matter how unlikely, where a fish might be holding. Every flat spot in a run of broken water is worth a cast or two. The long pools, perfectly formed for fish holding in the tailwaters, fish resting in the fat middle, fish feeding at the head, require a strategy. I stretch out on a warm flat rock to reconnoiter the situation, reconsider my fly pattern, give the fish a chance to forget about whatever noise I made in getting there.

Hours pass. The river goes on forever, or at least I haven't fished to the end of one yet. If I am aware of time at all, it is through noises in my stomach and then through the diminishing light in the sky. I will be in a little trouble by now. Yet it would be the same if I were the one with the folding chair and the book. I would disappear into the pages of that book and stay inside for as long as it took, coming out the other end fresh from another world, fresh from a kind of dream, renewed and awakened. On a good day, fishing is just like that.

I woke up this morning to a guy on the radio suggesting I draw a triangle and label the corners "faster," "better," and "cheaper." He told me I could not simultaneously do anything faster, better, and cheaper, that I must recognize this universal human limit and cover one corner of my triangle. All day I walked around with my head buzzing. How, I wondered, could anything outside the realm of competitive athletics be both faster and better? Or in any realm, cheaper and better? I understood "faster" and "cheaper," but didn't understand why I would want to do anything in such a way, or own anything made under these conditions. But I see "faster" and "cheaper" is becoming the axis of this spinning world.

The world pushes for greater velocity. All the time, I am expected to move faster than my natural inclination. Fax machiners, e-mailers want my answer, and they want it now. I need time to think, to consider my options. My students can become an impatient rabble. It seems like when I was in college my professors took weeks to return my papers. Now my students are unhappy if I don't have them ready at the next class meeting. I long for quietitude. The long afternoons I used to sink into books have somehow shrunken away. Hours themselves have grown shorter, pass faster, as yet another deadline looms up on my pocket calendar.

Owning a motorcycle was a way of going with the high-speed flow; I see that now. Without really meaning to, I would find myself going eighty miles an hour between stoplights. Only after I let that bike go did I admit how much faster it was than I would ever be. One day it would have taken me where I didn't want to go in its quick, simple-minded way, and I would have been unable to do anything but follow. Together, we were an accident waiting to happen. I got a letter from the Division of Motor Vehicles telling me just that after I got three speeding tickets in six months. I sold the motorcycle. But I still must remind myself I ought to slow down since speeding in a car remains my greatest sin against slowness. It's the one way I can try to catch up with the day's events and expectations. A foolish way, and the best justification for selling the bike and doing all I can to avoid filling my life up with any more internal combustion engines.

I label my own triangle "slower," "better," and, since in America time is always money, "more expensive." Seen in this way, fishing is my most natural activity. But not the float fishing my father preferred. Sitting with a bobber and worm is too slow even for me. And not spin fishing. Casting a spinner or a spoon turns it into a projectile, and projectiles move too fast. Fly-fishing was made for my slowness.

When I first tried a graphite fly rod, I couldn't get used to it. It was shorter and quicker than the fat fiberglass rods I had fished with for over twenty years. My back cast kept getting as far as it needed to go faster than I was ready for it to. So I dropped my back cast. And I didn't know to open my stance and watch the line travel in flight. The Scout merit badge book just showed silhouettes of a boy with his rod cocked at ten o'clock and one.

There is another good reason for watching my back cast. It helps me keep my mind on casting. I don't think this is a problem for the quick. A quick person full of efficient action must fill up his brain with making motion, whereas I move slowly enough that I find myself with time to think between every motion. After I have been out fishing for a while, my mind wanders in the middle of a cast. Suddenly I catch myself thinking about any old thing while my fly hits the water behind me, or, depending on when the stray thought strikes me, while my rod carries too far forward, my line piles up in front of me, and the cast fizzles.

If slowness is to fulfill all its promise, it must be taken on with total concentration. This is what I mean when I say that I sometimes forget the heart of fishing is learning to wait. Casting a dry fly is the truest exercise of slowness I know. First, I must lift my rod tip, lift my line off the water. I bring the tip up over my head and the line picks itself up, something like a long skinny camel standing up and coming right along behind my rod, shaking off water, following reluctantly. Then, just behind my head, I stop the rod, and stopping is a hard part because it's such a pleasure to set a rod and line in motion. It's such a pleasure to watch a long pennant unfurl back behind me, I'd like to

see it go on forever. Some time between forever and now, longer than you would expect, longer than a quick, impatient person is willing to wait, the line reaches its almost end. Nobody's eyes are fast enough to see this moment, though some people think theirs are. I know even as I watch my line pay out that I'll be guessing, going on what I think I see and what I trust to feel. It is in these long pauses, hundreds and thousands of them on a satisfying fishing day, that the brain has time to remake itself, to empty out and fill back up again in a fresh and renewed sort of way.

I start my rod forward and the line, just now reaching its end, turns on itself and obediently comes along. Now is the time, as the line runs out ahead of me, to stop and wait again, to resist driving the rod forward and ruining the cast by trying to make it go farther than it was meant to, to let the leader play out with a last little flutter so that the fly drops to the water in the same loopy way a real bug might. I wait one last time while the fly rides on its course determined by the water, traveling as far as it can go before being pulled under by the current or skating against the resistance of the line. Anything can happen when a fly is on the river. A fish will pick its moment; sometimes a fly will have just touched the surface. Sometimes a fly may be within inches of my leg when a fish finally takes it. Most times, no fish rises. The trick in waiting is to be open for the fish that will rise. In this way, the slow passage of the fly down the river can be seen to take no time at all.

There is a price for the luxury of slowness. Books and magazines pile up around me faster than I can read them. Lists of places I intend to fish grow longer. I just can't seem to get to all these rivers and lakes in the time I have. But isn't it better to read fewer books, reading each with the care it deserves? Isn't it better to give a good fishing hole the attention it deserves? In this way, a few river miles might take a lifetime to know well. In this way, I take in the world at the pace I can best absorb it. In this way, I fall farther behind.

But a hurried day on the river is a ruined one. Too often, I find myself making a pledge to the clock and heading off upriver. I'm taking seven-league strides in my waders, scaring the fish out of pools three bends away because I have to get out there and use what time I have. I tie on a fly and make a series of sloppy casts. I'm trying to work some line into play and cast to a good spot at the same time and wind up doing neither. Then when I don't get a fish, I rush to the next hole. When I raise no fish there, I begin swapping my fly every dozen casts or so, begin shifting from drys to nymphs on the flimsiest of impulses. I don't have time to look for whatever bugs might be on the river, but every time I change flies I'm made to look at my watch. And I see that time too is striding along in big twenty-minute and half-hour intervals. When my fishing time is up, I will be well away from the truck, false casting as I come down the river, laying my fly in this spot and that one, never leaving it long enough to have a full drift. But that doesn't matter since I'm fishing the river bassackwards anyhow and splashing more than ever.

What in this world can be better done in a hurry? Surely, some things can be done more quickly. I envy people who can turn out a nicely tied dry fly in ten or fifteen minutes, those who tie sure, fast knots. I envy those who react to a rising fish always just in time. But when I try quickness, I get a tangled-up rush. The fly I tie is a mess not worth fishing, the knot must be redone. And I miss the fish too often by anticipating its strike. When I'm in a rush, I make less of the little time I do have. Ill-considered choices are compounded by careless actions. Hurrying becomes a useless, self-defeating strategy. Hurrying is denying the truth of my slowness.

I wish I could say the bamboo fly rod has solved all my problems. It remains true to Howie's prediction, slow. It is, as the guy in Texas said in his high-handed way, heavy. Yet most days it feels right, which means it feels slow, and slow is what I come by naturally. I like the slow arcing flex of the rod, bending well into the middle section. It must take more time for such a rod to bend and unbend itself, to let go of its power and put it into the line. I like to think I feel it in my long boney arms.

No fishing rod can solve my problem. My problem is the world itself that has so little understanding of and places so little value on slowness. Sometimes I feel like I am forever wading upriver against a fairly stiff current, picking up one foot, testing my balance, stepping, bringing the other foot up beside it. Waiting before the next step while time keeps pushing against me. While waiting, I am looking to see the indignant squirrel up the spruce tree, for the prospect of some blueberries on the bank, moose tracks in the soft silt. Maybe a fish under the cut bank. No matter how slow I go, the sun ticks across the sky indifferent to my pace. It's helpful to remember that.

"He sure is missing
a lot of fun,"
the cowboy said.

OBITUARY WITH BAMBOO FLY ROD

Here's a story Dave Stark told me. Once he and another guy drove over Murphy Dome to do some fishing on the lower Chatanika. On the west side of the dome the road drops down into a permafrost bog. That's where they got balled up in the mud on that one-lane road too skinny to turn around in. Equipped with nothing but an axe and a come-along, they spent the better part of an Alaska summer day pulling themselves out of the muck and yanking the truck around in the road for the trip back over the dome. I'm not sure if they did any fishing at all.

I used to teach high school English in a little town in piedmont Carolina, a little town that lies along the road from the Charlotte airport to my parents' home in Virginia. There, in my very first year of teaching, I taught a boy who was clearly smarter than I was. I saw his quickness instantly, the way he probed a short story and came out with things, made connections that none of the other kids quite saw, that I saw but had to admit I wouldn't have thought of myself. Because I was a new teacher, I didn't have the self-assurance or presence of mind to see that at least I had the edge in simple knowledge. I taught this young man for three years, coached him in cross-country, led him on hikes with the outing club. When I moved on to graduate school, I started a short list, the kind of list I wonder if all teachers don't secretly keep, of the truly gifted, of those marked for some future distinction. For a few years he remained the only one on that list, and I waited for his name to turn up in the newspaper, maybe in the book reviews or academic journals. I was sure it would turn up somewhere so that even way over in Alaska I would detect the ripple.

That's the kind of information I'm on the lookout for when I read the paper, the little connections that assure me that through a messy web of tangles the world is held together. Everybody scans the paper for the big stuff—who's bombing whom, further proof of what scoundrels we've elected to high office—but I want to get around that to the revelations of the human heart also to be found right there in the daily newspaper. For this reason I must read both "Dear Abby" and "Ann Landers"; the features on outstanding local school-children; the sports page, with particular emphasis on the compiled statistics of hometown leagues and results of local foot, dog sled, and automobile races; the announcements of engagements, weddings, and births; the letters to the editor; the court judgments; and the police blotter.

There in the police blotter on a dark day deep in the bottom of winter, among the requisite petty thieveries, DWIs, and collisions, I saw a report of a man found dead in his apartment, dead of a gunshot wound. Foul play was not suspected, but I wasn't mystified. I know how to read the evasive language of the police report.

I know the spot on the lower Chatanika that Dave Stark was headed for. I know the road up the Fairbanks side of Murphy Dome. The road leads to my house, but to get to the river you'd go past my turn and on up the dome. Toward the top, the road flattens out and you can see you're pretty much above the tree line and into tundra. Some willow shoots line the road, but behind them are big patches of blueberries and low bush cranberries. In the late summer we come here to pick those berries, especially in the fields just below the Air Force radar installation. And if that place is too crowded or over-picked, we will go out the road onto the saddle below the dome. From there the road drops off toward the Chatanika River and Minto Flats beyond. Which is why, they say, this road to almost nowhere exists. A state senator wanted a quicker way to get out to the Flats for his bird hunting, his moose hunting, his pike fishing, than driving all the way around to the far side, to New Minto Village off the Elliot Highway.

This state was rich then. Putting a rough road through with a couple of Caterpillar tractors and a heavy road grader so a senator and his buddies could more conveniently slip away to the real Alaska was no big deal. Alaska isn't so rich now, and that senator is dead. The road has deteriorated. I wouldn't try it except in a truck with four-wheel drive. I always remember to carry a come-along and an axe too.

I found the rest of the story of the dead man a few days later when

I read another part of the paper I read daily without fail, the obituaries. A modern obituary is often a stingy bit of reportage; nobody wants to get too close to revealing the cause of their grief. This one was more forthcoming than most. The dead man was older than I was, though not by much. He would have been a senior in high school when I was a freshman, one of the big guys who punched freshmen in the arm, who smoked behind the gym, had a girl and his own car. And he was one who wound up in Vietnam whether he intended to or not.

It might be too easy to imagine that nothing went right from there. He had a string of jobs—policeman in two states, sold cars and was good at it, mined gold, worked for the Bureau of Land Management. Left a couple of wives, a couple of kids in different states. Most recently he lived with yet another woman. Maybe he gave up on the durability promised by a ceremony. And maybe at the end as he died of cancer, as death became more inevitable and life more painful, neither she nor anybody else could do anything to help him.

The obituary says he owned a bamboo fly rod, his grandfather's old rod, his grandfather from back in Missouri. I lived down in Arkansas for a while where the runoff from the fertilizer and chicken litter had ruined the fish for eating. So maybe I envied the people up in Missouri where the water ran cold and clear out from the bottoms of hydroelectric dams and made the fishing for trout good year-round. I wondered how it was then, when his grandfather must have caught rainbows as long as your arm fishing the tailwaters down from the sluice gates. That would have been before the editors of fishing magazines started running feature stories, the kind where a fisherman in waders kneels before the camera offering up a subdued and weighty fish in his outstretched arms. And I wondered what it was to come to own such a fine fishing rod, a rod that had some fishing in it, and I considered why, in the end, it wasn't enough.

Sometimes a thing comes into your hands without its history attached. Sometimes you have to figure it out by yourself. After it's been used a while, a bamboo rod can take a set, a noticeable bend in the tip section of the rod. A casting set, its tip bending upward, is an indication of many more casts than fish taken, and a fighting set means a rod took its share of big fish, fish that took something out of the rod. My own bamboo rod arrived without a casting or a fighting set. It said very little of who had owned it except that perhaps one day he put it up wet and stored it carelessly. The steel guides rusted through their wraps; the varnish crazed.

Shouldn't it be otherwise? Shouldn't the elegant old thing come dragging the past behind it? When I am on the riverbank with my bamboo rod in hand, I want to stand in the present and look back into a past that leads not only inevitably to this moment, but to the rightness of this moment. Norman Maclean might think so, too. I've read in *A River Runs Through It* where he says nobody ought be allowed to catch a fish off a bad cast. To think such a thing is to believe in the rightness of nature, or in the case of Mr. Maclean, to believe in the complicity of God with nature, God lurking in the background to make sure things come out right.

And I think, what about accidents? Accidents, for example, like the one where I overshoot my cast and it flips up around a twig hanging over the river, swinging just a minute before it slithers off and into a river. Maybe a fish has caught a glint off the hook and is rising to take the fly even as it falls. And I think if we're going to disallow that catch, then what about fish caught on poorly tied flies, caught on flies tied in Third World countries by underpaid peasants? Fish caught on cheap outfits that are an insult to the art of fishing or fish caught on overpriced ones bought by the vainglorious who think a brand name says something about their human worth. If you took those reasons into account, who among us has caught many fish worth mentioning?

Among the stories I took up with my high school students was Joseph Conrad's "Heart of Darkness." It is not a particularly easy story to get across in a high school classroom. I found myself taking my students through it one sentence at a time in places, feeling a little like the narrator Marlow himself chugging up an unknown river—always against the current—in his steamer. It was a worthwhile trip for me, if only because I taught myself something I'd managed never to see clearly in four years as an English major at a pretty good school. Here were great paragraphs. Here were paragraphs that ran sentences by the reader like rivers of words, sometimes rushing, sometimes majestic and barely seeming to move at all. Here was a skill you could spend your life trying to grab onto.

And my student, the smart one on my very short list, saw Conrad's genius too, though he thought for a minute it might be me. "The man really knows how to read this stuff," he told a bunch of other kids as one class pushed out the door against the next one coming in. Still, I was relieved. I thought I had taught him something useful.

There is a need in all of us, I think, to believe the world is somehow ordered. In the river there are fish. Even if our eyes are good, we rarely see them, yet we cast into the pools to the spots where we expect them to be holding. The flies we use are often the flies we used the last time the light was like this, the water this high, the season right about now. Often this method works. We cast, and sure enough, just like last year, there's a fish rising, revealing itself.

One afternoon, driving my brother's car home to see the folks, I took the exit off the interstate, drove into town and up the main street divided by the little-used railroad tracks, took the right on Center Street, and parked in front of the school where I had taught. Maybe it was ten years, maybe fifteen. But everything was just as it was, the same school secretary, my friend the physics teacher still in his same room, still at his desk grading some tests or lab reports. I sat down in a student desk and pretty soon many of the other teachers I had known came by. My ex-uncle-in-law was there and so the talk turned to my other ex-in-laws and where they were and how they were doing. Which saddened and embarrassed me, to think that a whole part of my life had sheered off and drifted away from me like an iceberg. Rick came up, my ex-brother-in-law, as smart and mulish a man as I've ever known. I believe I'd like him still, though I'll bet he's gone Republican on me.

"He was our only Morehead Scholar," somebody said. And I said, no, my student had been a Morehead Scholar too.

"You know what happened to him, don't you?"

"No." And I believe I wanted to know.

"He killed himself." Nobody knew why. That's too bad, we all said; that's a shame. But we were friends who hadn't seen each other in a long time, so our talk moved on.

It's hard not to blame myself. That's another secret list I suspect most teachers have—the list of all the mistakes you make, all the things you could have done differently, said differently, or never said at all. It's one thing when the guy you sent to the principal's office once a week knocks over a gas station; it's another when it's a kid off your short list. Here was a kid with the world rolling out in front of him, just waiting for him to walk in it, to make a piece of it his own. What went wrong? And what could I have said or done that would have stopped it?

How to be? That's what Conrad really wants to know. That's what I sometimes worry that Norman Maclean wants to come at a little too easily, something having to do with his Presbyterianism. God is out there and has the whole thing planned out. Except there's the central problem of *A River Runs Through It*, the wonderfully gifted brother, dead of another kind of self-destruction. Despite the rich, assuring language of Mr. Maclean's closing paragraphs—the river has cut through the rock as ordained for ages—the brother's death stands as a senseless, unnecessary act. Death cannot be reconciled despite a wash of words. How, then, to be?

In the obituary before me, I read that our man has been awarded three Bronze Stars for valor and a Purple Heart. You'd think that would be lesson enough. You'd think that having steamed upriver with Marlow, my student would have seen the horror of a life

Lisa Woodward 1995

unraveled. You'd think lessons learned at such young ages would wrap themselves around a person like a magic girdle, making these men somehow immune from failures at marriage, failures at work, from accrued disappointments. If not immune from disease, then immune from the humiliation, the degradation of constant pain and physical decline.

At its tip, a well-made bamboo fly rod is about the diameter of the lead in a wooden pencil. Six sections of split, planed, and tapered cane have been fitted together so as to appear a single piece of wood. A picture of a good fisherman caught at the end of his back cast will show the butt of the rod upright and barely passing beyond the perpendicular line made by his body. But the upper section of the rod will be well bent, trailing behind with the line almost like an elongated pennant. Despite the great force brought to bear on it, as near as I can tell, such a rod can't really be worn out.

For a while, though, that's why I thought bamboo rods came with two tips, that somehow you could fish the life out of one. But it turns out this isn't so. Most bamboo rods get their tips snapped off in car doors, against tree trunks, under the feet of careless or clumsy fishermen.

One of the most satisfying experiences you can have as a teacher is for one of your old students to look you up. Just to say hello, just so you can see he's doing OK in this world. Jeff was stubborn and absentminded. A long-distance runner and cyclist with out-of-the-way interests for a high school boy in cooking and sewing. Now he was a cowboy, a real one, and a ferrier and a saddle maker. I took a look at the pictures of his leather work, the English and western saddles, and saw in the clean sure lines that he'd grown himself a sense of style. The saddles were elegant, functional things.

Our talk turned, as I knew it would, to my student on the short list, and of course Jeff knew about the same facts I did. Maybe it was his job, maybe his marriage. We were back to saying another round of too bads. Only this time we were eating Italian food in Alaska when it was twenty below outside. "He sure is missing a lot of fun," the cowboy said.

Well, yeah. We fly-fish in the pouring rain, ski in the freezing cold, when anybody with sense would sit home by the fire. We invite pain and discomfort into our lives. And I guess I do it in part for practice. So that on the days when pain and discomfort come unbidden and won't go away, I will have somehow prepared myself.

I have no confidence this trick will work. If it did, the suasive powers of writers like Joseph Conrad and Norman Maclean would be enough to make us all look into our souls and come up better for it. We'd come to know badness for what it is and stay away from it. The fly-caster's four-count beat would be a kind of mantra for us all, suggesting a mechanism for a life of precision and control. Our ethical behavior would grow naturally from the beauty of these writers' words.

It's been a few years since I've fished the lower Chatanika, the place where Dave Stark got bogged down. I've decided I don't much like to fish that spot. You come out on the river at a long, flat pool, a good place to launch a boat, but no use to a fisherman without one. Upriver is an island and on its west side is a deep hole promising all sorts of fish. I've tried it with dry fly, wet fly, nymph, and streamer, and never taken a fish out of it. There are two hundred yards or so of good water just above that hole where big fish can be found in the late fall. And beyond that, more straight water where sometimes a fish or two can be had. But there are no compelling fishing problems here, no sweepers hanging over the river, no riffles to channel the current, no combination of tricky turns and rocky hiding places that make a spot a fishing revelation. And there is the road. That muddy track through permafrost looks to be a clean shot to the river as you approach it from the saddle above. But every year it makes itself more a pathless wood, a muddy bog that can leave you far from the river with no chance of turning back.

How to be? For that poor guy holding onto his grandpa's bamboo rod, full of bright promises of clear water and big fish, it somehow was not enough to preserve him. A mistake, maybe, to think the objects of this world have talismanic qualities. Having the old man's rod, we think we have his experience, his wisdom. Maybe we do if we look at it another way. The rod cannot say what wisdom grandpa had. It can only be a tool in your hand. You can fish with it through good days and bad. If you know how to find fish and know how to cast with it, the rod will help you catch them. You can use it, and maybe learn some things for yourself.

I take to the river in the last good days of fall. The leaves are yellow and dropping, but the river is still full of life. Bugs are rising, and the fish are following them to the surface. In the quiet, I cast and hear my line rattle through the guides as my own bug settles on the water. Soon it will be cold; the fish will regard my flies from the river's bottom with lazy suspicion. Here are days; there won't be any others.